The Path of Light: Unlocking the Secrets of the Pyramid Texts

The Path of Light: Unlocking the Secrets of the Pyramid Texts

By Ancient The Architect

Copyright and Disclaimer Page

Copyright © 2025 by Ancient The Architect
Published by Health Is Luxury
All rights reserved.

No part of this publication may be reproduced, stored in a retrieval system, or transmitted in any form or by any means—electronic, mechanical, photocopying, recording, or otherwise—without the prior written permission of the publisher, except in the case of brief quotations used in critical reviews and other non-commercial uses permitted by copyright law.

This book is a work of creative interpretation and metaphysical exploration based on the *Pyramid Texts*. While every effort has been made to ensure accuracy in historical and spiritual content, the interpretations provided are the author's own and are intended to serve as a bridge between ancient wisdom and modern metaphysical perspectives.

Disclaimer

The information in this book is provided for educational and spiritual purposes only. It is not intended to replace professional advice in any field, including but not limited to legal, medical, psychological, or financial matters. Readers are encouraged to seek professional consultation for specific issues requiring expertise.

The metaphysical commentary in this book reflects the author's interpretations and is not an official representation of ancient Egyptian religious or cultural practices. The publisher and author make no warranties or representations about the accuracy, completeness, or suitability of the content for any purpose. Any reliance you place on the material is strictly at your own risk.

This book is intended to honor the legacy of ancient Egypt by presenting its teachings in a way that is meaningful and relevant to contemporary readers. The interpretations and applications are offered as tools for personal growth and spiritual alignment.

Published by: Health Is Luxury

ISBN: 979-8-9922102-5-5

First Edition: 2025
Printed in the United States of America

Table of Contents

Preface

- The Pyramid Texts: More Than a Collection of Ancient Spells
- A Timeless Roadmap for Spiritual Evolution and Ascension

The Pyramid as a Map of Consciousness

- Introduction to the 13-Step Framework
- Progression from Earthly Limitations to Divine Unity
- The 13 Steps as Portals to Ascension

Chapter 1: A 13-Step Path to Ascension

1. The Call to Awaken
2. Confronting the Threshold
3. Activating the Divine Word
4. Traversing the Waters
5. Awakening the Sacred Fire
6. Walking the Path of Ma'at
7. Entering the Void
8. Awakening Divine Vision
9. Ascending Through Unity
10. The Resurrection of Light
11. The Crown of Cosmic Wisdom
12. The Throne of Eternal Union
13. The Infinite Cycle

Concluding Word: The Eternal Sun

Chapter 2: Framework for the Metaphysical Deployment of the 25 Spells

1. Power Over Enemies
2. Protection
3. Opening the Way
4. Divine Nourishment
5. Mastering Chaos
6. Ascension
7. Illumination
8. Journeying Through the Sky
9. Resurrection and Rebirth
10. Joining the Divine Council
11. Harmonization
12. Eternal Renewal
13. Divine Ascension
14. Navigating the Celestial Rivers
15. Uniting with Ancestral Wisdom
16. Mastering the Shadow
17. Reclaiming Divine Authority
18. Harmonizing the Divine Spheres
19. Unlocking the Hidden Gates
20. Eternal Renewal
21. Empowering the Ka
22. Sacred Union
23. Mastering Cosmic Law
24. Eternal Radiance
25. Unity with the Source

The Sacred Journey of the SUNs of God

- The Journey in Stages
- Practical Integration
- Metaphysical Translation of the Resurrection Ritual Your Role as a SUN of God
- Final Affirmation

Preface

The **Pyramid Texts** offer more than a collection of ancient spells; they provide a timeless roadmap for spiritual evolution and ascension. These texts, carved into the walls of pyramids during Egypt's Old Kingdom, are among the world's oldest religious writings, consisting of approximately **800 spells or utterances**. Originally intended to guide the deceased pharaohs on their journey to the afterlife, they encompass a wide range of spiritual themes, from protection against danger to the attainment of divine wisdom.

This book does not aim to reinterpret all of the utterances found in the Pyramid Texts. Instead, it presents a carefully selected and adapted collection of **25 spells**, grouped into categories to provide practical guidance for spiritual seekers today. Through the metaphysical breakdown of these adapted spells, the SUNs of God are equipped to navigate the challenges, revelations, and transformations of their sacred journey.

Each spell acts as a tool, guiding the seeker toward higher realms of consciousness and unity with the divine source. Whether facing fear, seeking wisdom, or striving for divine illumination, these ancient teachings remind us that the journey is as eternal as the soul itself.

As you engage with these metaphysical interpretations, let them inspire you to look within, honor the light you carry, and embrace your role as a SUN of God. The path of ascension is not linear but cyclical, a spiral that leads ever closer to the infinite source. May these insights empower you to rise, transform, and shine as beings of divine truth and love.

The Pyramid as a Map of Consciousness

The Pyramid Texts, etched into the walls of the ancient pyramids, serve not only as a guide for the pharaoh's journey to the afterlife but also as a blueprint for the soul's ascension into higher planes of consciousness. Each hieroglyph and invocation offers encoded wisdom for navigating the mysteries of the self, aligning with universal truths, and realizing the eternal nature of the soul.

This work reinterprets the Pyramid Texts through a metaphysical lens, revealing their hidden messages for spiritual awakening. The 13 steps outlined here reflect the soul's progression from earthly limitations to divine unity, offering practical and esoteric insights into transforming consciousness. Each step is a portal, a threshold through which the seeker confronts challenges, integrates wisdom, and ascends toward higher states of being.

Chapter One: A 13-Step Path to Ascension

Step 1: The Call to Awaken – Recognizing the Divine Spark

Metaphysical Insight

The journey begins with a single realization: you are more than a physical being. The Pyramid Texts repeatedly emphasize the pharaoh's divine nature, reminding us that the first step to ascension is recognizing the divine spark within ourselves. The texts often invoke Ra, the Sun God, as the ultimate source of light and life, symbolizing the eternal presence of divine consciousness.

This step corresponds to the awakening of the inner eye—the spiritual realization that one is not bound by material existence but is a fragment of the infinite. The hieroglyphs depicting the rising sun and the ascension of Ra are metaphors for this inner awakening, urging the seeker to rise from the slumber of ignorance and see themselves as a radiant being of light.

Intellectual Analysis

In academic terms, this step parallels the concept of **gnosis**, or direct experiential knowledge of the Divine. The Pyramid Texts invite us to shift our focus from external rituals to inner recognition. The frequent mentions of "rising," "light," and "ascension" are not merely about physical movement but signify the elevation of consciousness from mundane concerns to spiritual awareness.

The invocation of divine names and powers at this stage reflects the activation of latent spiritual energies. Each deity represents an aspect of the self that must be awakened to begin the journey.

Practical Application

- **Meditation on Light**: Visualize the sun rising within your heart, radiating light throughout your being. Reflect on the question: *What divine spark within me is waiting to be ignited?*
- **Affirming the Divine Nature**: Speak aloud an affirmation rooted in the essence of the texts: *I am a child of light, destined to rise and unite with the infinite source.*

This practice prepares the seeker to move forward, awakening the dormant aspects of their consciousness and opening the pathway to higher realms.

Step 2: Confronting the Threshold – The Guardians of Duality

Metaphysical Insight

The second step involves confronting the guardians of the spiritual threshold. The Pyramid Texts describe numerous protective deities and serpentine figures that guard the sacred passageways. These entities are symbolic of the dualities within us: fear and faith, ignorance and wisdom, materiality and spirituality.

To proceed, the seeker must balance these forces, recognizing that the guardians are not external foes but reflections of their inner doubts and unresolved conflicts. The invocation of Ma'at, the goddess of truth and balance, signifies the need for harmony as the key to unlocking the gates of consciousness.

Intellectual Analysis

From a metaphysical perspective, this stage is akin to the alchemical **solve et coagula**—dissolving old structures to integrate higher truths. The Pyramid Texts describe the guardians as testing the pharaoh's resolve, echoing the psychological process of confronting the ego's resistance to change.

This stage also emphasizes the principle of **ascent through challenge**: spiritual growth occurs not by avoiding obstacles but by transmuting them into stepping stones. The serpents symbolize the kundalini energy that rises when the seeker harmonizes duality within themselves.

Practical Application

- **Self-Inquiry**: Identify one fear or limiting belief that acts as a guardian at your spiritual threshold. Reflect on how this fear can be transformed into a source of strength.
- **Visualization**: Imagine standing before a sacred gate, flanked by serpents of light. Each serpent represents a duality you must integrate. Visualize yourself walking confidently through the gate as the serpents bow in acknowledgment of your inner balance.

Step 3: Activating the Divine Word – The Power of Sacred Speech

Metaphysical Insight

The Pyramid Texts place profound emphasis on the spoken word, often invoking "utterances" to activate divine power. This step reveals that the spoken word is not merely sound but a vibrational force capable of shaping reality. To ascend, the seeker must align their speech with divine truth, understanding that each word carries the essence of creation.

The invocation of sacred names in the texts reflects the ability to harmonize the self with divine forces through speech. These utterances awaken dormant aspects of the soul and connect the seeker to higher realms. The "words of power" mentioned are metaphors for divine alignment, where thought, intention, and speech converge to manifest spiritual reality.

Intellectual Analysis

In the context of metaphysical traditions, this step aligns with the **Logos**—the creative principle of the universe. The Pyramid Texts depict sacred names as bridges between the human and divine realms, emphasizing the power of intentional articulation.

Psychologically, this stage represents the refinement of internal dialogue. The seeker must eliminate self-defeating patterns of speech and replace them with affirmations that resonate with their highest potential. Each spoken word becomes an instrument of transformation, directing the energy of the soul toward ascension.

Practical Application

- **Sacred Name Invocation**: Choose a name or phrase that represents your highest ideal (e.g., "Light Eternal" or "Truth Divine"). Speak it aloud with intention, feeling the vibrations ripple through your being.
- **Word Purification**: For one day, observe your speech. Eliminate any words that reflect doubt, fear, or negativity. Replace them with words of affirmation and purpose.

By aligning your words with the divine, you become a co-creator of higher realities, embodying the creative principle that flows through all existence.

Step 4: Traversing the Waters – Emotional Cleansing and Renewal

Metaphysical Insight

The Pyramid Texts frequently refer to sacred waters as sources of purification and renewal. Traversing these waters symbolizes the cleansing of emotional residue and the preparation of the soul for higher ascension. The waters of the Duat are not mere rivers; they represent the subconscious mind, where unresolved emotions and past experiences are stored.

This stage calls the seeker to release attachments, heal emotional wounds, and embrace forgiveness. Just as water flows and adapts, the soul must learn to navigate emotional currents with grace, allowing them to transform rather than overwhelm.

Intellectual Analysis

Metaphysically, water is the universal symbol of emotion, intuition, and spiritual renewal. The Pyramid Texts suggest that these waters are not external but flow within the seeker. The process of traversing them mirrors **emotional alchemy**, where raw emotions are transmuted into wisdom and compassion.

The texts' repeated mention of Ra's journey through watery realms reflects the soul's resilience and adaptability. The waters represent challenges that cleanse and purify, preparing the soul to carry the light of truth into deeper mysteries.

Practical Application

- **Reflection on Emotional Currents**: Spend time journaling about emotions that feel unresolved. What patterns or attachments need to be released for renewal?
- **Water Ritual**: Fill a bowl with water, symbolizing emotional cleansing. Place your hands over it and visualize releasing negativity into the water. Pour the water away, imagining your emotions flowing freely and harmoniously.

This step reminds the seeker that emotional mastery is a gateway to spiritual liberation, clearing the path for higher vibrations to enter.

Step 5: Awakening the Sacred Fire – Transforming Through Will

Metaphysical Insight

The Pyramid Texts often invoke images of fire, portraying it as both a destroyer of impurities and a beacon of transformation. This sacred fire represents divine will, the inner power that propels the soul through challenges and trials. To ascend, the seeker must embrace this fire as a force of renewal, burning away limiting beliefs and igniting the passion for spiritual truth.

The guardians of this stage test the seeker's resolve, presenting fears and doubts to be consumed in the purifying flames. The fire symbolizes the awakening of spiritual will, which is necessary to overcome inertia and embody divine purpose.

Intellectual Analysis

In metaphysical traditions, fire is a symbol of **transmutation** and the creative spark of the divine. The Pyramid Texts describe fiery entities as both protectors and purifiers, illustrating the dual role of challenges as catalysts for growth.

This step corresponds to the activation of the **solar plexus**, the energy center governing willpower and personal transformation. The fire within is not destructive but illuminative, bringing clarity and purpose to the soul's path.

Practical Application

- **Visualization of Sacred Fire**: Close your eyes and imagine a golden flame at the center of your being. Feel it growing stronger, consuming fears and energizing your spirit with divine will.
- **Daily Action of Will**: Choose one small but meaningful action that aligns with your spiritual purpose. Complete it with focus and determination, knowing it fuels your ascent.

By embracing the sacred fire, the seeker transforms challenges into opportunities for growth, becoming a radiant vessel of divine light.

Step 6: Walking the Path of Ma'at – Living in Divine Balance

Metaphysical Insight

The concept of Ma'at, the goddess of truth and cosmic order, is central to the Pyramid Texts. To ascend, the seeker must embody her principles, aligning thoughts, actions, and intentions with universal harmony. Ma'at's scales symbolize the balance required to navigate spiritual pathways, where every step is measured against the soul's alignment with truth.

This stage is not merely about external morality but about internal equilibrium. The seeker learns to balance light and shadow, intuition and reason, and the individual will with divine will. Walking the path of Ma'at is an ongoing practice of self-accountability and alignment.

Intellectual Analysis

Ma'at represents **cosmic justice**, the natural order that sustains creation. The Pyramid Texts often depict the weighing of the heart against the feather of Ma'at, a metaphor for living in harmony with divine principles.

This stage parallels the metaphysical concept of **balance as power**—where the soul's strength lies in its ability to hold opposing forces in harmony. The invocation of Ma'at reflects the soul's commitment to unity and truth.

Practical Application

- **Daily Reflection**: At the end of each day, reflect on your actions. Were they aligned with your highest truths? What adjustments can you make to live more harmoniously?
- **Living the Feather**: Carry a small feather as a reminder to act with lightness, truth, and balance. Let it guide your decisions throughout the day.

Walking the path of Ma'at prepares the soul for the higher stages of ascension, where alignment with divine order becomes the foundation for unity with the source.

Step 7: Entering the Void – Embracing the Unknown

Metaphysical Insight

The Pyramid Texts often refer to the mysterious void, a realm where form dissolves and the soul confronts the infinite potential of the unknown. This stage symbolizes the surrender of ego and the embrace of divine mystery. To progress, the seeker must step into the void without fear, trusting in the unseen forces that guide transformation.

The void is not a place of loss but of profound creation, where the soul's old patterns dissolve, making way for higher vibrations. This is the space where divine intelligence operates beyond the confines of the material world, and the seeker learns to trust the wisdom of the cosmos.

Intellectual Analysis

Metaphysically, the void represents **liminality**, a transitional space where old identities and attachments are released. The Pyramid Texts describe the void as a realm of darkness, yet it is pregnant with light and new possibilities.

Psychologically, entering the void reflects the process of surrendering control, letting go of certainty, and embracing the unknown as a sacred teacher. It mirrors the archetype of death and rebirth, where the ego dies to allow the soul to ascend to higher states of being.

Practical Application

- **Meditative Surrender**: Spend time in meditation focusing on the concept of nothingness. Envision yourself floating in a vast, dark void, completely supported and at peace.
- **Symbolic Release**: Write down a fear or attachment you are ready to release. Burn the paper in a safe space, visualizing the void transforming it into light.

By entering the void, the seeker aligns with the flow of divine intelligence, emerging renewed and ready for higher stages of consciousness.

Step 8: Awakening Divine Vision – Seeing Beyond the Material

Metaphysical Insight

The Pyramid Texts emphasize the importance of sight and vision as divine attributes. This stage represents the awakening of spiritual sight, where the seeker begins to perceive the hidden realities behind the material world. It is here that the soul develops intuitive clarity and the ability to discern the divine patterns woven into existence.

This awakening is not about physical sight but the activation of inner vision, allowing the seeker to access higher truths and understand their role within the cosmic order. It is a stage of profound revelation and alignment with divine purpose.

Intellectual Analysis

In metaphysical traditions, the awakening of divine vision corresponds to the activation of the **third eye** or the seat of intuitive knowledge. The Pyramid Texts describe the "opening of the eyes" as a moment of cosmic insight, where the soul sees the interconnectedness of all things.

This stage is also a test of perception, challenging the seeker to look beyond illusions and see the divine essence in all experiences. It requires clarity, focus, and trust in one's intuitive faculties.

Practical Application

- **Visualization of Light**: Close your eyes and imagine a radiant light shining from the center of your forehead. This light reveals hidden truths and illuminates your path.
- **Journaling Practice**: Reflect on a time when your intuition guided you toward a higher understanding. What did you learn, and how can you strengthen this connection?

Awakening divine vision allows the seeker to move through the spiritual journey with clarity, seeing beyond surface appearances to the divine truth within.

Step 9: Ascending Through Unity – Embracing Oneness

Metaphysical Insight

The Pyramid Texts describe moments of profound unity, where the soul merges with divine forces and ascends to higher realms of consciousness. This stage represents the transcendence of duality and the realization that all existence is interconnected.

To ascend, the seeker must embrace oneness, dissolving the illusion of separation between self and other, physical and spiritual, finite and infinite. This stage is the culmination of the soul's efforts, where divine union becomes the primary reality.

Intellectual Analysis

Unity is a central theme in many metaphysical systems, reflecting the **non-dual nature** of existence. The Pyramid Texts portray this as the merging of the soul with Ra, symbolizing the eternal connection between the individual and the divine.

This stage is not a destination but a realization, where the seeker understands that unity has always been present. The soul's journey through the previous stages prepares it to fully embody this truth, transforming life into an expression of divine harmony.

Practical Application

- **Meditation on Unity**: Imagine yourself as a drop of water merging into a vast ocean. Feel the boundaries between yourself and the universe dissolve.
- **Daily Acts of Unity**: Perform one act each day that reminds you of your interconnectedness with others—whether through kindness, gratitude, or collaboration.

By embracing unity, the seeker transcends the limitations of individuality, becoming a vessel for divine expression.

Step 10: The Resurrection of Light – Becoming a Beacon

Metaphysical Insight

The Pyramid Texts frequently refer to the resurrection of the SUN as a metaphor for the soul's triumph over darkness. This stage represents the soul's emergence as a radiant beacon of divine truth, carrying the light of higher consciousness into the world.

This is a stage of empowerment, where the seeker not only embodies divine wisdom but shares it with others, inspiring them to embark on their own journeys of ascension. It is the moment where personal transformation becomes a source of collective upliftment.

Intellectual Analysis

The resurrection of light corresponds to the **realization of spiritual mastery**, where the soul integrates all lessons and becomes a conscious co-creator with the divine. The Pyramid Texts emphasize that this light is not separate from the seeker but an inherent aspect of their being, waiting to be fully expressed.

This stage is also a reminder of the cyclical nature of the journey, where the resurrection of light leads to new beginnings and further exploration of divine mysteries.

Practical Application

- **Sharing Your Light**: Reflect on how your spiritual journey has shaped you. Identify one way you can share your insights or gifts with others to inspire their growth.
- **Daily Practice of Radiance**: Begin each day by visualizing yourself as the rising SUN, spreading light, warmth, and positivity to all you encounter.

The resurrection of light is not the end but a new beginning, where the seeker becomes a guiding star for others on the path.

Step 11: The Crown of Cosmic Wisdom – Embodying Divine Intelligence

Metaphysical Insight

At this stage, the seeker ascends to the realm of cosmic wisdom, symbolized in the Pyramid Texts as the ultimate enlightenment and divine understanding. Here, the soul transcends the limits of mortal thought and aligns with the intelligence of the cosmos. This stage represents the activation of the higher mind, where divine will and individual consciousness operate in perfect harmony.

The Crown of Cosmic Wisdom reflects the soul's capacity to access universal truths and integrate them into its earthly existence. It is a state of alignment with the eternal laws that govern creation, where the soul becomes a living embodiment of divine intelligence.

Intellectual Analysis

In metaphysical terms, this stage corresponds to the **crown chakra**, the energetic center that connects the individual to higher planes of consciousness.

The Pyramid Texts suggest that wisdom is not simply acquired but realized through union with the divine. This wisdom is inherently cosmic, encompassing the principles of harmony, balance, and eternal truth.

Psychologically, the crown represents the culmination of the soul's journey, where all lessons are integrated, and the seeker embodies their divine potential. The soul no longer seeks knowledge externally but understands that true wisdom arises from within.

Practical Application

- **Meditative Connection**: Visualize a golden crown of light above your head, symbolizing your connection to divine intelligence. Imagine this light flowing through you, illuminating your mind and heart.
- **Living Wisdom**: Reflect on one universal truth that resonates deeply with you. Commit to living in alignment with this truth in your daily actions.

By embodying cosmic wisdom, the seeker becomes a channel for divine intelligence, serving as a bridge between heaven and earth.

Step 12: The Throne of Eternal Union – Returning to the Source

Metaphysical Insight

The final stage of the journey is the throne of eternal union, where the soul merges completely with the divine source. This stage is often depicted in the Pyramid Texts as the return to Ra, the cosmic life force that sustains all existence. The throne symbolizes the soul's rightful place within the cosmic order, where it experiences unity with the eternal.

This union is not an end but a return—a recognition that the soul has always been part of the divine and that the entire journey has been about remembering this truth. The throne represents mastery, fulfillment, and the eternal cycle of ascension.

Intellectual Analysis

Eternal union reflects the non-dual nature of existence, where the seeker realizes there is no separation between self and the divine. The Pyramid Texts describe this as the ultimate reward for the soul's trials—a state of eternal harmony and peace.

In this state, the soul transcends all illusion, entering a realm where individuality dissolves into cosmic unity. The throne is both a seat of sovereignty and a symbol of surrender, where the seeker simultaneously claims their divine inheritance and relinquishes all attachment to ego.

Practical Application

- **Visualization of Unity**: Imagine yourself seated on a radiant throne, surrounded by infinite light. Feel this light merging with your essence, erasing all boundaries between you and the divine.
- **Daily Reminder**: Begin and end each day with the affirmation, "I am one with the eternal source." Allow this truth to guide your thoughts and actions.

The throne of eternal union is the culmination of the soul's journey—a state of infinite love, wisdom, and harmony that transcends all boundaries.

Step 13: The Infinite Cycle – Beyond the Journey

Metaphysical Insight

The Pyramid Texts remind us that the soul's journey is eternal. Even after reaching the throne of union, the process of growth, learning, and ascension continues. The infinite cycle reflects the dynamic nature of consciousness, where every ending is a new beginning.

This step emphasizes the cyclical nature of spiritual evolution, where the soul revisits stages of the journey, each time ascending to greater heights. The infinite cycle is not about completion but about continuous expansion, where the soul becomes a co-creator with the divine.

Intellectual Analysis

The concept of infinite cycles aligns with the metaphysical principle of **eternal progression**, where consciousness evolves perpetually. The Pyramid Texts illustrate this through imagery of the SUN's daily rise and fall, symbolizing the soul's ongoing journey through light and darkness.

This stage teaches that spiritual mastery is not static but dynamic, requiring the seeker to embrace change, growth, and renewal as eternal truths.

Practical Application

- **Gratitude for the Journey**: Reflect on the steps you have taken in your spiritual journey. Write down three lessons that have shaped you and express gratitude for the growth they brought.
- **Commitment to Growth**: Set an intention to approach each new challenge as an opportunity for expansion, trusting in the infinite wisdom of the divine.

By embracing the infinite cycle, the seeker aligns with the eternal flow of life, where every moment is an opportunity for divine expression.

Concluding Words: The Eternal SUN

The Pyramid Texts reveal the soul's journey as a sacred process of transformation, ascension, and union with the divine. Each stage offers profound insights into the nature of consciousness, guiding the SUNs of God toward their ultimate realization as divine beings.

This 13-step process is not a linear path but a dynamic framework that reflects the eternal nature of spiritual growth. As the SUN rises and sets, so too does the soul journey through light and darkness, continually expanding its understanding of the cosmos and its place within it.

The Pyramid Texts remind us that the journey is as important as the destination. Every challenge, every revelation, and every step brings the seeker closer to their divine essence. Through this sacred process, the SUNs of God become radiant beacons of light, illuminating the path for all who seek to remember their eternal nature.

Chapter Two: Framework for the Metaphysical Deployment of the 25 Spells

1. Power over Enemies: Conquering Inner and Outer Obstacles

The **Spells for Power over Enemies** are designed to empower the soul to overcome resistance, both internal and external. In the Pyramid Texts, enemies often symbolize forces of chaos, ignorance, and fear that obstruct spiritual progress. These spells equip the SUNs of God with the tools to assert divine authority and maintain alignment with Ma'at (cosmic order).

Key Spells and Metaphysical Interpretation:

- **The Binding of Set (Unis, West Wall)**
  Metaphysical Purpose: Set, representing chaos, is a metaphor for the disruptive forces within the soul, such as doubt, anger, or fear. This spell asserts the soul's dominance over such energies, ensuring harmony prevails.
  Application: When experiencing inner conflict or external challenges, <u>visualize binding the chaos within you using threads of divine light.</u> Affirm your alignment with universal order.

- **Annihilating the Serpent Apep (Teti, East Corridor)**
  Metaphysical Purpose: Apep, the serpent of darkness, embodies the soul's deepest fears. This spell provides the seeker with tools to dissolve illusions and face shadow energies.
  Application: During moments of fear or uncertainty, imagine wielding a divine weapon (e.g., a staff or sword of light) to pierce the serpent's form, turning darkness into radiant light.

- **Sealing the Enemies of Ra (Pepi I, North Gallery)**
  Metaphysical Purpose: This spell ensures that negative forces—be they inner doubts or external obstacles—cannot disrupt the divine journey. It symbolizes the protection of the soul's sacred mission.
  Application: Invoke this spell during spiritual work or challenging situations by mentally sealing your energetic field with golden light. <u>Visualize Ra's presence surrounding you as a shield.</u>

Deployment: Phrases and Symbolism

While the Pyramid Texts often include incantations or invocations for these spells, we metaphysically interpret the deployment of these tools through visualization, affirmation, and energetic alignment:

- <u>Visualize the act of binding, piercing, or sealing as an energetic transformation.</u>
- Invoke the archetypes of Ra, Ma'at, or divine light to symbolize higher power assisting your actions.
- Focus on the intention of restoring balance and harmony, both within and without.

Practical Insight for Power Over Enemies:

The **Spells for Power over Enemies** remind the SUNs of God that true power lies in mastering internal chaos. By confronting fear and doubt with clarity and intention, the soul strengthens its resolve, ensuring that nothing diverts it from its divine path.

2. Protection: Safeguarding the Divine Light

The **Spells of Protection** ensure the soul's safe passage through the trials of the Duat, shielding it from harmful forces and preserving its divine essence. These spells invoke sacred guardians, cosmic symbols, and divine energies to ward off negativity.

Key Spells and Metaphysical Interpretation:

- **The Four Pillars of Shu (Unis, First Threshold)**
  Metaphysical Purpose: The pillars represent the foundational principles that hold up the heavens and protect the soul from chaos.
  Application: <u>Visualize yourself surrounded by four luminous pillars, symbolizing stability, strength, and divine support.</u> Use these pillars as anchors during moments of doubt or fear.

- **Invoking the Eye of Horus (Teti, Protective Seal)**
  Metaphysical Purpose: The Eye of Horus is a symbol of vigilance and divine power. It restores balance and ensures that no harm comes to the soul.

Application: When facing challenges, imagine the Eye of Horus glowing above you, dispelling darkness and revealing the path forward. Affirm your alignment with divine protection.

- **The Guardian Serpent of Ra (Pepi II, Guardian Chamber)**
  Metaphysical Purpose: The serpent, as a sacred protector, symbolizes kundalini energy awakened for defense and ascension.
  Application: In meditation, imagine a radiant serpent coiling around you, its energy forming a protective shield while uplifting your consciousness.

Deployment: Phrases and Symbolism

- Symbols such as pillars, eyes, and serpents serve as visual anchors.
- Affirmations could include: ***"I am divinely protected by the light of Ra and the guardians of truth."***
- Deploy these spells during times of fear, uncertainty, or spiritual attack by visualizing divine guardians surrounding you.

Practical Insight for Protection:

The **Spells of Protection** remind the SUNs of God that safety is not external but arises from their connection to divine forces. By invoking these spells, the soul anchors itself in trust and alignment, ensuring its passage through the challenges of transformation.

3. Opening the Way: The Threshold of New Beginnings

The **Spells for Opening the Way** are rites of passage, clearing obstacles and granting the soul access to higher realms. They are crucial for the SUNs of God to initiate their journey with clarity and intention.

Key Spells and Metaphysical Interpretation:

- **The Way of Wepwawet (Unis, Pathway of Stars)**
  Metaphysical Purpose: Wepwawet, the "Opener of the Ways," symbolizes divine guidance through uncharted territories.
  Application: At the start of any new endeavor, invoke Wepwawet by visualizing a golden path unfurling before you, lit by divine light. Affirm your readiness to walk the sacred path.

- **Unlocking the Gates of the Horizon (Teti, Solar Portal)**
  Metaphysical Purpose: This spell symbolizes the soul's ability to

transcend limitations and enter higher states of consciousness.
Application: During meditation, imagine a radiant gate opening before you. Step through with confidence, leaving behind all doubts and fears.

- **Clearing the Path of Ma'at (Pepi I, Hall of Harmony)**
  Metaphysical Purpose: Aligning with Ma'at ensures the journey is grounded in truth and harmony.
  Application: Reflect on areas of your life where truth needs to prevail. Align your actions with cosmic harmony to clear inner and outer blockages.

Deployment: Phrases and Symbolism

- Visualize pathways, gates, and cosmic horizons.
- Affirmations such as: *"The way is open before me; I walk in alignment with divine truth."*
- Use these spells at the beginning of new chapters in life, during rituals for clarity, or when seeking direction.

Practical Insight for Opening the Way:

The **Spells for Opening the Way** empower the SUNs of God to embrace new beginnings with faith and alignment. They remind us that every journey begins with a single step, guided by divine light.

4. Divine Nourishment: Sustaining the Soul's Strength

The **Spells for Divine Nourishment** provide spiritual sustenance to the soul, ensuring it has the vitality and resilience needed to traverse the trials of the Duat. These spells align the seeker with the life-giving forces of the cosmos.

Key Spells and Metaphysical Interpretation:

- **Consuming the Bread of Ra (Unis, Solar Banquet)**
  Metaphysical Purpose: The bread symbolizes divine wisdom that sustains the soul's journey.
  Application: In moments of spiritual fatigue, <u>visualize yourself partaking in a sacred banquet</u>. Feel the nourishment of divine wisdom filling your being.

- **Drinking the Waters of Nun (Pepi II, Fountain of Life)**
  Metaphysical Purpose: The primordial waters of Nun represent the source of all life and renewal.

Application: During meditation, imagine drinking from a fountain of pure, radiant water. Feel its vitality restoring your soul's strength.

- **Receiving the Fruit of Isis (Teti, Garden of Eternity)**
  Metaphysical Purpose: The fruit represents the nurturing power of the divine feminine, offering guidance and sustenance.
  Application: <u>Visualize receiving a glowing fruit from Isis, its energy filling you with clarity, intuition, and courage.</u>

Deployment: Phrases and Symbolism

- Symbols like bread, water, and fruit can represent nourishment.
- Affirmations such as: ***"I am nourished by divine wisdom and sustained by eternal light."***
- Use these spells during periods of exhaustion, doubt, or when seeking spiritual replenishment.

Practical Insight for Divine Nourishment:

The **Spells for Divine Nourishment** remind the SUNs of God that sustenance is not only physical but spiritual. By aligning with these cosmic energies, the soul gains the vitality to continue its transformative journey.

5. Mastering Chaos: Conquering the Serpent of Disorder

The **Spells for Mastering Chaos** equip the soul to confront and overcome the forces of disorder, symbolized by the serpent Apep. These spells emphasize the soul's power to restore balance and ascend beyond the reach of chaos.

Key Spells and Metaphysical Interpretation:

- **Binding the Serpent of Apep (Pepi I, Chamber of Balance)**
  Metaphysical Purpose: Apep represents inner chaos and fear; binding it symbolizes reclaiming mastery over these forces.
  Application: In moments of doubt or turmoil, <u>visualize yourself wielding a golden cord to bind the serpent of fear.</u> Affirm your power over disorder.

- **Calling on Sekhmet's Flame (Teti, Hall of Fire)**
  Metaphysical Purpose: Sekhmet's flame burns away illusions, leaving only truth and clarity.

Application: Imagine a blazing fire surrounding you, incinerating fear and doubt. Step forward with renewed courage and clarity.

- **Restoring the Balance of Ma'at (Unis, Scales of Truth)**
  Metaphysical Purpose: This spell reaffirms the soul's alignment with cosmic order, neutralizing the effects of chaos.
  Application: Reflect on areas of imbalance in your life and take steps to restore harmony through deliberate action.

Deployment: Phrases and Symbolism

- Use imagery of fire, cords, and scales to visualize conquering chaos.
- Affirmations such as: ***"I master the forces of chaos, restoring harmony within and around me."***
- Apply these spells during moments of inner conflict or external disorder.

Practical Insight for Mastering Chaos:

The **Spells for Mastering Chaos** empower the SUNs of God to confront inner and outer discord with courage and clarity. By neutralizing the serpent of fear, the soul moves closer to divine balance.

6. Ascension: Rising Beyond the Physical Realm

The **Spells for Ascension** represent the soul's ability to rise above earthly attachments and embrace its divine essence. These spells guide the SUNs of God to transcend material limitations and ascend to higher planes of consciousness.

Key Spells and Metaphysical Interpretation:

- **The Ladder of Ra (Unis, Celestial Climb)**
  Metaphysical Purpose: The ladder symbolizes the soul's ascent toward divine light, where each rung represents a step closer to unity with the Source.
  Application: <u>Visualize a golden ladder stretching from the earth to the heavens.</u> With each breath, ascend a rung, leaving behind the weight of earthly concerns.

- **The Wings of Horus (Pepi II, Flight of the Falcon)**
  Metaphysical Purpose: The wings of Horus signify spiritual freedom and the ability to rise above challenges

with clarity and purpose.
Application: During meditation, imagine yourself growing radiant wings. Feel them lifting you toward divine realms, free from limitations.

- **The Seat of Osiris (Teti, Throne of Eternity)**
  Metaphysical Purpose: Osiris's throne represents divine authority and the soul's rightful place in the cosmic order.
  Application: <u>Visualize yourself seated on a glowing throne of light, embodying your divine sovereignty.</u> Affirm your alignment with cosmic laws.

Deployment: Phrases and Symbolism

- Visualize ladders, wings, or thrones to embody ascension.
- Affirmations such as: ***"I rise above all earthly attachments, ascending to my divine essence."***
- Use these spells during moments of spiritual expansion or when seeking to overcome material concerns.

Practical Insight for Ascension:

The **Spells for Ascension** remind the SUNs of God that their true nature is not bound to the physical realm. By ascending in consciousness, they align with divine truths and become beacons of light for others.

7. Illumination: Revealing the Hidden Light

The **Spells for Illumination** awaken the soul to hidden truths, unveiling the divine light within. These spells emphasize clarity, insight, and the power of spiritual vision.

Key Spells and Metaphysical Interpretation:

- **Unveiling the Eye of Ra (Unis, Divine Gaze)**
  Metaphysical Purpose: The Eye of Ra represents divine perception, cutting through illusion to reveal ultimate truth.
  Application: In quiet contemplation, visualize the Eye of Ra opening within you, illuminating all that was hidden. Let its light guide your decisions and insights.

- **Lighting the Flame of Sia (Teti, Torch of Wisdom)**
  Metaphysical Purpose: Sia, the deity of perception, symbolizes the inner flame of understanding that lights the path forward.
  Application: Picture a torch igniting within your heart, its flame growing

brighter as your wisdom deepens. Affirm your alignment with divine clarity.

- **Revealing the Hidden Stars (Pepi I, Celestial Mapping)**
  Metaphysical Purpose: The stars symbolize divine guidance, reminding the soul of its place in the cosmos.
  Application: Imagine a night sky filled with radiant stars, each representing a piece of divine wisdom. Allow their light to guide you through moments of uncertainty.

Deployment: Phrases and Symbolism

- Use imagery of eyes, torches, and stars to embody illumination.
- Affirmations such as: ***"The divine light within me reveals all truth and wisdom."***
- Deploy these spells during times of confusion or when seeking deeper spiritual clarity.

Practical Insight for Illumination:

The **Spells for Illumination** empower the SUNs of God to see beyond the veil of illusion. They teach that light is not something to seek outside but a divine presence to be uncovered within.

8. Journeying through the Sky: Ascension and Navigation

These spells empower the SUNs of God to navigate higher realms with precision and grace. In the Pyramid Texts, the sky is not just a physical space but a spiritual dimension representing expanded awareness and connection to the divine.

Key Spells and Metaphysical Interpretation:

- **Opening the Gates of Heaven (Teti, North Wall)**
   Metaphysical Purpose: This spell symbolizes the opening of higher dimensions. The gates represent access to spiritual realms where wisdom and guidance reside.
   Application: In meditation, visualize a radiant gateway opening before you. Step through with confidence, affirming your readiness to receive divine insight.

- **Flying to the Imperishable Stars (Pepi II, Sky Ritual)**
  Metaphysical Purpose: This spell represents the soul's liberation from earthly confines, ascending to a realm of eternal light and truth.
  Application: During moments of spiritual ascent, imagine yourself as a bird or beam of light soaring toward the stars. Feel yourself merging with their eternal energy.

- **Navigating the Celestial Boat (Unis, West Gable)**
  Metaphysical Purpose: The celestial boat symbolizes the soul's ability to traverse spiritual realms under divine guidance. This spell ensures smooth passage through these dimensions.
  Application: <u>Visualize yourself aboard a golden boat, steered by divine beings.</u> Feel the calm waters beneath and the starlit sky above as you journey to higher consciousness.

Deployment: Phrases and Symbolism

- Visualize gates, stars, or boats as metaphors for spiritual access and guidance.
- Use affirmations like: ***"I ascend to realms of light, guided by divine wisdom,"*** to focus your intent.
- During meditation, imagine celestial beings (e.g., Ra or Nut) accompanying and blessing your journey.

Practical Insight for Journeying through the Sky:

The **Spells for Journeying through the Sky** teach that ascension is not a departure but a deeper connection to universal truth. The soul learns to navigate the spiritual cosmos, embracing its role as a co-creator with the divine.

9. Resurrection and Rebirth: The Soul's Renewal

The **Spells for Resurrection and Rebirth** guide the SUNs of God through the process of shedding the old and embracing a renewed state of being. These spells focus on the soul's emergence from the trials of the Duat (Underworld) into the light of a new day, symbolizing spiritual transformation and eternal life.

Key Spells and Metaphysical Interpretation:

- **Rising as the Morning Star (Pepi II, Sunrise Chamber)**
  Metaphysical Purpose: This spell represents the soul's triumph over darkness and its rebirth into divine light. The Morning Star is a metaphor for renewed hope and purpose.
  Application: At dawn or a moment of renewal, <u>visualize yourself as a radiant star rising on the horizon.</u> Affirm your commitment to spiritual growth and your role as a beacon of light.

- **Reviving the Body of Osiris (Unis, Central Passage)**
  Metaphysical Purpose: This spell reflects the soul's ability to regenerate its spiritual essence, much like Osiris is revived to symbolize renewal and eternal life.
  Application: During spiritual practices, <u>visualize your body, mind, and spirit being infused with divine energy.</u> Imagine yourself merging with Osiris, embodying resilience and regeneration.

- **Emerging from the Lotus (Teti, Sacred Pool)**
  Metaphysical Purpose: The lotus symbolizes purity and enlightenment. This spell represents the soul's rise above the murky waters of the past, untouched and radiant.
  Application: In meditation, imagine yourself as a lotus blossom opening to the sunlight. Feel the petals of your consciousness unfolding, revealing your highest self.

Deployment: Phrases and Symbolism

- Use imagery such as stars, lotus flowers, or the sunrise to represent personal renewal.
- Affirmations could include: ***"I rise renewed, embodying the eternal light of divine truth."***
- Engage in rituals like cleansing baths or sunrise meditations to symbolize rebirth.

Practical Insight for Resurrection and Rebirth:

The **Spells for Resurrection and Rebirth** remind the SUNs of God that every challenge is an opportunity for renewal. By embracing change and letting go of what no longer serves, the soul aligns with its eternal essence, emerging stronger and more radiant.

10. Joining the Divine Council: Accessing Higher Wisdom

These spells focus on the soul's integration into the divine order, symbolized by joining the company of gods. The Pyramid Texts often describe the deceased as sitting among the divine council, embodying their wisdom and power.

Key Spells and Metaphysical Interpretation:

- **Sitting Among the Netjeru (Pepi I, Assembly Hall)**
  Metaphysical Purpose: This spell affirms the soul's equality with divine beings, symbolizing mastery and alignment with cosmic order.
  Application: In meditation, <u>visualize yourself seated among divine figures.</u> Feel their wisdom infusing your being, affirming your role as a co-creator with the divine.

- **Receiving the Crown of Ra (Teti, Coronation Ritual)**
  Metaphysical Purpose: The crown represents divine authority and the acknowledgment of the soul's ascension to a higher state.

Application: Imagine a radiant crown of light being placed on your head, signifying your alignment with divine will. Affirm your readiness to embody this responsibility.

- **Speaking the Words of Ma'at (Pepi II, Judgment Chamber)**
  Metaphysical Purpose: This spell empowers the soul to speak and act in harmony with universal truth, becoming a vessel for divine wisdom.
  Application: Reflect on moments when your words or actions can bring harmony to a situation. Speak intentionally, aligning with principles of truth and justice.

Deployment: Phrases and Symbolism

- Use visualizations of divine councils, crowns, or symbols of Ma'at to embody wisdom and authority.
- Affirmations such as: ***"I am a vessel of divine wisdom, speaking truth and embodying cosmic harmony."***
- Apply these spells during decision-making or when seeking higher guidance.

Practical Insight for Joining the Divine Council:

The **Spells for Joining the Divine Council** teach the SUNs of God that ascension is not a solitary journey but one of collaboration with higher forces. By aligning with divine wisdom, the soul becomes a conduit for universal truths, contributing to the cosmic order.

11. Harmonization: Balancing the Divine Energies

The **Spells for Harmonization** bring the SUNs of God into alignment with universal rhythms and cosmic truths. These spells focus on balance—between light and dark, masculine and feminine, material and spiritual—and the integration of dualities within the self.

Key Spells and Metaphysical Interpretation:

- **Balancing the Scales of Ma'at (Unis, Cosmic Harmony)**
  Metaphysical Purpose: The scales represent the universal law of balance and justice, urging the soul to align with divine truth.
  Application: Reflect on situations in your life where balance is needed. <u>Visualize Ma'at's feather on one scale and your heart on the other.</u> Feel the peace that arises when balance is restored.

- **The Harmony of the Twin Lions (Pepi II, Solar Alignment)**
  Metaphysical Purpose: The twin lions symbolize the balance between past and future, urging the seeker to remain present.
  Application: During meditation, visualize two lions guarding a golden gate. Step through this gate into the present moment, releasing attachment to time and duality.

- **The Sacred Union (Teti, The Divine Marriage)**
  Metaphysical Purpose: The union of divine polarities, such as Ra and Hathor, reflects the integration of masculine and feminine energies within.
  Application: <u>Visualize the sun and moon merging into one radiant orb, embodying unity.</u> Affirm your balance between action and receptivity.

Deployment: Phrases and Symbolism

- Visualize scales, lions, or orbs to align with harmony.
- Affirmations such as: ***"I embody the balance of divine energies, uniting dualities within myself."***

- Use these spells when seeking peace, resolution, or alignment in chaotic circumstances.

Practical Insight for Harmonization:

These spells teach that harmony is not static but dynamic, requiring conscious effort to balance forces within and without. They guide the SUNs of God to live as vessels of cosmic balance, embodying universal principles.

12. Eternal Renewal: Cycles of Rebirth

The **Spells for Eternal Renewal** highlight the cyclical nature of existence, emphasizing the soul's ability to continuously regenerate and rise anew. They empower the seeker to release what no longer serves and embrace each moment as an opportunity for rebirth.

Key Spells and Metaphysical Interpretation:

- **The Phoenix Flame (Unis, Sacred Ashes)**
  Metaphysical Purpose: The phoenix represents renewal through destruction, teaching that endings are gateways to new beginnings.
  Application: <u>Visualize yourself as a phoenix rising from its ashes,</u> shedding old patterns and limitations. Affirm your readiness for transformation.

- **The Well of Eternal Youth (Pepi I, Waters of Life)**
  Metaphysical Purpose: The sacred well symbolizes the eternal flow of life, reminding the soul of its infinite potential.

Application: <u>Visualize drinking from a glowing well of water, feeling its vitality flowing through your body and spirit.</u>

- **The Resurrection of Osiris (Teti, The Green Renewal)**
  Metaphysical Purpose: The rebirth of Osiris represents the soul's power to regenerate and align with divine will, no matter the obstacles.
  Application: Envision yourself as Osiris, reborn from the embrace of the earth. Let the green fields of renewal inspire your inner growth.

Deployment: Phrases and Symbolism

- Use imagery of flames, wells, and green fields for renewal.
- Affirmations such as: ***"I am continuously renewed, embracing each moment as an opportunity for rebirth."***
- Deploy these spells during times of personal growth, transition, or reinvention.

Practical Insight for Eternal Renewal:

These spells guide the SUNs of God to see life as an unending cycle of growth, reminding them that even in darkness, the seeds of renewal are planted.

13. Divine Ascension: Reaching the Highest Realms

The **Spells for Divine Ascension** represent the culmination of the soul's journey, where the SUNs of God achieve unity with the source. These spells focus on transcendence, guiding the soul to its ultimate destination in the divine light.

Key Spells and Metaphysical Interpretation:

- **The Path of the Rising Sun (Pepi II, Solar Ascent)**
  Metaphysical Purpose: The sun's journey upward mirrors the soul's return to divine truth and eternal light.
  Application: <u>Visualize the rising sun illuminating your path,</u> guiding you to higher realms of understanding and peace.

- **The Starry Path of Nut (Unis, Celestial Bridge)**
  Metaphysical Purpose: Nut, the sky goddess, symbolizes the infinite expanse of divine consciousness. Her starry body serves as a bridge to the divine.

Application: <u>Visualize yourself walking along a celestial bridge,</u> each star a stepping stone toward divine union.

- **The Throne of Ra (Teti, Seat of Divine Power)**
  Metaphysical Purpose: The throne signifies the soul's return to its rightful place in the divine order, embodying sovereignty and enlightenment.
  Application: <u>Visualize yourself seated on a radiant throne, crowned with light, fully aligned with universal truth.</u>

Deployment: Phrases and Symbolism

- Visualize suns, stars, and thrones for ascension.
- Affirmations such as: ***"I ascend to the highest realms, merging with the infinite light of the divine."***
- Use these spells during moments of spiritual culmination or transcendence.

Practical Insight for Divine Ascension:

The **Spells for Divine Ascension** remind the SUNs of God that the ultimate goal is unity with the source. These spells empower the soul to rise above all limitations, embracing its eternal nature.

14. Navigating the Celestial Rivers: The Flow of Divine Energy

The **Spells for Navigating the Celestial Rivers** encapsulate the soul's journey across the vast, cosmic waterways of the afterlife. These spells invoke imagery of sacred rivers, stars, and divine vessels to symbolize the flow of spiritual energy and trust in higher guidance. For the SUNs of God, these passages emphasize surrender, allowing oneself to be carried by divine currents toward enlightenment and renewal.

Key Spells and Metaphysical Interpretation:

- **The Sacred Barque of Ra (Pepi I, Divine Vessel):**
    - **Metaphysical Purpose:** This spell invokes Ra's barque as a vehicle of divine guidance, symbolizing safe passage across the celestial waters. It represents trust in divine will and the soul's ability to surrender to higher currents.

- **Application:** <u>Visualize yourself aboard Ra's radiant barque, traveling smoothly across cosmic rivers.</u> Feel the flow of divine energy steering your course toward enlightenment.
- **The River of Stars (Unis, Pathway of Illumination):**
    - **Metaphysical Purpose:** This spell uses the imagery of celestial rivers filled with stars, symbolizing infinite opportunities for spiritual insight. Each star acts as a point of illumination, guiding the soul.
    - **Application:** Imagine floating on a river of stars, their light reflecting your own divine potential. Allow each glimmer to awaken a new understanding.
- **The Wellspring of Renewal (Teti, Fountain of Rebirth):**
    - **Metaphysical Purpose:** The wellspring symbolizes emotional purification and the rejuvenation of the soul. By connecting to this source, the soul renews its vitality.

- **Application:** <u>Visualize a fountain of pure, radiant light flowing through your being, cleansing all doubts and fears, and recharging your spirit.</u>

Deployment: Phrases and Symbolism

- Invoke divine guidance by meditating on the barque of Ra.
- Use affirmations such as: ***"I surrender to the divine currents, trusting the flow of my spiritual journey."***
- Symbols include water, stars, and vessels, reflecting fluidity and movement through divine realms.

Practical Insight for Navigating Celestial Rivers:
The Spells for Navigating the Celestial Rivers teach the SUNs of God to embrace the flow of divine energy. This stage emphasizes trust, surrender, and alignment with the higher currents of existence, reminding the seeker that divine guidance is ever-present.

15. Uniting with Ancestral Wisdom: The Eternal Continuum

The **Spells for Uniting with Ancestral Wisdom** emphasize the profound connection between the living and those who came before. These spells serve as a bridge, linking the seeker with an eternal lineage of divine intelligence and guidance. For the SUNs of God, this connection is not only a source of strength but also a reminder of their place within a continuum of light, wisdom, and purpose.

Key Spells and Metaphysical Interpretation:

- **The Ancestral Throne (Pepi II, Seat of Knowledge):**
    - **Metaphysical Purpose:** This spell calls upon the wisdom of those who came before, emphasizing the soul's connection to a continuum of divine intelligence.
    - **Application:** <u>Visualize yourself seated among luminous ancestors, absorbing their collective wisdom and integrating it into your being.</u>

- **The Ancestral Bridge (Unis, Gateway of Connection):**
  - **Metaphysical Purpose:** This spell emphasizes the interconnectedness of all beings across time and space, creating a bridge between the earthly and divine realms.
  - **Application:** Imagine crossing a radiant bridge where you exchange knowledge and blessings with ancestors, merging their insights with your own spiritual growth.
- **The Pillars of Light (Teti, Beacons of Guidance):**
  - **Metaphysical Purpose:** These pillars symbolize the unwavering support of divine and ancestral forces, lighting the way forward.
  - **Application:** Meditate on radiant pillars surrounding you, each representing an ancestral force or guiding principle that strengthens your journey.

Deployment: Phrases and Symbolism

- Invoke ancestors through rituals or meditations honoring their legacy.
- Use affirmations such as: ***"I am the living expression of ancestral wisdom, guided by their eternal light."***
- Symbols include bridges, thrones, and pillars, reflecting stability and connection.

Practical Insight for Uniting with Ancestral Wisdom:

The Spells for Uniting with Ancestral Wisdom remind the SUNs of God that they are never alone. The wisdom of the ancestors flows through them, empowering their journey toward divine realization.

16. Mastering the Shadow: Embracing Inner Duality

The **Spells for Mastering the Shadow** guide the SUNs of God through the profound journey of self-discovery, where light and shadow are brought into balance. These spells emphasize the importance of confronting hidden aspects of the self, transforming them into sources of wisdom and power. This sacred work of embracing duality is essential for achieving wholeness and unlocking the full potential of the soul.

Key Spells and Metaphysical Interpretation:

- **The Mirror of Truth (Pepi I, Reflection of the Soul):**
    - **Metaphysical Purpose:** This spell reveals the shadow self, challenging the soul to integrate its hidden aspects. It represents self-acceptance and the power of transformation.
    - **Application:** Stand before a metaphorical mirror and confront your shadow with compassion. Acknowledge its lessons and integrate its energy into your journey.

- **The Binding Serpent (Unis, Tamer of Chaos):**
    - **Metaphysical Purpose:** This spell uses the serpent as a symbol of chaos, which must be tamed and redirected into creative potential.
    - **Application:** <u>Visualize taming a coiled serpent, its energy transforming into a radiant force that empowers your spiritual path.</u>
- **The Flame of Transmutation (Teti, Purifier of Intentions):**
    - **Metaphysical Purpose:** Fire symbolizes the purging of impurities, enabling the soul to rise above egoic tendencies.
    - **Application:** Picture a divine flame burning away fear and doubt, leaving only the purified essence of your being.

Deployment: Phrases and Symbolism

- Use phrases that affirm mastery over the shadow, such as: *"I embrace all parts of myself, transforming shadow into light."*
- Symbols include mirrors, serpents, and flames, representing the transformative journey of inner duality.

Practical Insight for Mastering the Shadow:
The Spells for Mastering the Shadow teach the SUNs of God to embrace their full selves. By integrating light and shadow, the seeker achieves wholeness, unlocking untapped spiritual power.

17. Reclaiming Divine Authority: The Sovereign Soul

The **Spells for Reclaiming Divine Authority** focus on awakening the SUNs of God to their inherent divinity and rightful place within the cosmic order. These spells emphasize the balance of power with humility, reminding the seeker that true sovereignty arises from alignment with universal principles. By reclaiming their divine authority, the soul steps fully into its role as a co-creator with the divine.

Key Spells and Metaphysical Interpretation:

- **The Crown of Light (Pepi II, Symbol of Sovereignty):**
    - **Metaphysical Purpose:** The crown represents divine authority and spiritual mastery. It reminds the SUNs of God of their inherent divinity and rightful place in cosmic order.
    - **Application:** <u>Visualize yourself crowned with radiant light, embodying divine wisdom and leadership.</u> Feel the weight of responsibility and the empowerment it brings.

- **The Staff of Dominion (Unis, Instrument of Command):**
    - **Metaphysical Purpose:** This spell emphasizes the balance of authority with humility, where leadership arises from alignment with divine will.
    - **Application:** Meditate on holding a staff that channels divine energy, guiding your actions with clarity and justice.
- **The Throne of Truth (Teti, Seat of Ma'at):**
    - **Metaphysical Purpose:** The throne symbolizes the soul's alignment with truth and cosmic law. It represents stability, integrity, and harmony with universal principles.
    - **Application:** Picture yourself seated on a throne infused with Ma'at's essence, radiating balance and divine justice.

Deployment: Phrases and Symbolism

- Invoke divine sovereignty through affirmations such as: *"I reclaim my divine authority, acting with wisdom and love."*
- Use symbols like crowns, staffs, and thrones to embody leadership and balance.

Practical Insight for Reclaiming Divine Authority:
The Spells for Reclaiming Divine Authority remind the SUNs of God that true power comes from unity with divine will. This stage emphasizes the balance between personal mastery and collective service, urging the soul to lead with wisdom and compassion.

18. Harmonizing the Divine Spheres: The Cosmic Balance

The Spells for Harmonizing the Divine Spheres guide the SUNs of God in aligning with the universal principles of balance and unity. These spells emphasize the importance of Ma'at—the embodiment of truth and harmony—as the foundation of cosmic and personal equilibrium. By embracing these teachings, the seeker integrates their energies with the greater flow of existence, contributing to both inner and outer peace.

Key Spells and Metaphysical Interpretation:

- **The Scales of Ma'at (Pepi I, Keeper of Balance):**
    - **Metaphysical Purpose:** This spell invokes Ma'at's scales to weigh the heart against the feather of truth. It symbolizes self-accountability and the pursuit of harmony.
    - **Application:** Imagine standing before the scales, observing your heart being weighed. Reflect on areas of imbalance and affirm your commitment to truth.

- **The Cosmic Pillars (Unis, Foundation of the Realms):**
    - **Metaphysical Purpose:** The pillars represent the structural harmony of the universe, uniting the physical and spiritual planes.
    - **Application:** <u>Visualize yourself standing between two radiant pillars,</u> feeling their stabilizing force as they align your energies with cosmic order.
- **The Spiral of Unity (Teti, Dance of the Spheres):**
    - **Metaphysical Purpose:** This spell uses the spiral as a symbol of interconnectedness, where all realms and beings are part of a divine whole.
    - **Application:** Picture yourself moving through a spiral of light, each step deepening your awareness of the unity of existence.

Deployment: Phrases and Symbolism

- Use affirmations such as: ***"I align with the cosmic balance, creating harmony within and without."***
- Meditate on symbols like scales, pillars, and spirals to enhance feelings of equilibrium and unity.

Practical Insight for Harmonizing the Divine Spheres:
The Spells for Harmonizing the Divine Spheres encourage the SUNs of God to embody balance and interconnectedness. By aligning with cosmic harmony, the soul contributes to universal peace and order.

19. Unlocking the Hidden Gates: The Keys to Higher Realms

The **Spells for Unlocking the Hidden Gates** invite the SUNs of God to transcend limitations and access higher planes of existence. These spells emphasize the use of divine tools—keys, words of power, and celestial pathways—to unlock the hidden realms of consciousness. By engaging with these sacred practices, the seeker awakens to their infinite potential and the vast wisdom of the cosmos.

Key Spells and Metaphysical Interpretation:

- **The Key of Ra (Pepi II, Opener of Realms):**
    - **Metaphysical Purpose:** This spell unlocks hidden gates within the soul, granting access to higher planes of consciousness. It symbolizes the power of divine illumination.
    - **Application:** <u>Visualize holding a radiant key that opens a golden gate,</u> leading to realms of expanded awareness and understanding.

- **The Words of Power (Unis, Vibrations of Creation):**
    - **Metaphysical Purpose:** Words and sacred utterances act as metaphysical keys, unlocking the gates of divine wisdom and manifestation.
    - **Application:** Chant or meditate on sacred sounds, feeling their vibrations opening pathways within your consciousness.
- **The Gateway of Stars (Teti, Passage to Eternity):**
    - **Metaphysical Purpose:** This spell uses celestial imagery to guide the soul through stellar pathways, symbolizing infinite potential and divine guidance.
    - **Application:** Picture yourself stepping through a starry portal, each star igniting new realizations and connections.

Deployment: Phrases and Symbolism

- Chant sacred phrases or visualize keys unlocking gates within your soul.
- Use affirmations such as: ***"I hold the keys to divine realms, unlocking infinite wisdom within me."***
- Symbols include keys, gates, and stars, representing access to higher knowledge.

Practical Insight for Unlocking the Hidden Gates:

The Spells for Unlocking the Hidden Gates remind the SUNs of God that the journey to higher realms begins within. These spells empower the seeker to access divine truths and ascend to their highest potential.

20. Eternal Renewal: The Circle of Life

The **Spells for Eternal Renewal** guide the SUNs of God through the transformative cycles of life, death, and rebirth. These spells emphasize the soul's infinite journey, where each phase brings growth, renewal, and alignment with divine truth. By embracing the eternal nature of existence, the seeker finds strength in transformation and peace in the continuity of the cosmic order.

Key Spells and Metaphysical Interpretation:

- **The Serpent of Eternity (Pepi I, Ouroboros of Life):**
    - **Metaphysical Purpose:** The serpent biting its tail symbolizes the eternal cycle of life, death, and rebirth. It represents the soul's infinite nature.
    - **Application:** Visualize a radiant serpent encircling you, its continuous form reminding you of your eternal essence.

- **The Tree of Renewal (Unis, Roots of Immortality):**

  - **Metaphysical Purpose:** The tree represents the soul's growth through cycles, where its roots ground it in wisdom and its branches reach for divine light.
  - **Application:** Picture yourself as a tree, drawing strength from the earth and reaching upward, embracing each phase of growth and renewal.

- **The Phoenix Rising (Teti, Embodiment of Rebirth):**

  - **Metaphysical Purpose:** The phoenix rising from ashes symbolizes the soul's triumph over challenges, emerging renewed and empowered.
  - **Application:** <u>Visualize yourself as a phoenix,</u> shedding old limitations and soaring into a new chapter of spiritual evolution.

Deployment: Phrases and Symbolism

- Use affirmations such as: *"I am eternal, constantly renewed by the cycles of divine light."*
- Meditate on symbols like the serpent, tree, and phoenix to embody eternal renewal.

Practical Insight for Eternal Renewal:
The Spells for Eternal Renewal remind the SUNs of God that every ending is a beginning. By embracing the cycles of life, the soul continuously evolves, aligning more deeply with divine truth.

21. Empowering the Ka: Energizing the Divine Self

The Spells for Empowering the Ka focus on revitalizing the soul's vital essence, the Ka, which serves as a bridge between the physical and divine realms. These spells remind the SUNs of God that their energy is inexhaustible when connected to the eternal life force. By awakening and energizing the Ka, the seeker ensures spiritual resilience and alignment with cosmic vitality.

Key Spells and Metaphysical Interpretation:

- **The Invocation of Vitality (Pepi I, Awakening the Life Force):**
    - **Metaphysical Purpose:** This spell focuses on energizing the Ka, the soul's vital double, which sustains life and spiritual vigor. It connects the SUNs of God to their eternal source of energy.
    - **Application:** <u>Visualize a stream of golden energy flowing into your body,</u> filling your Ka with vitality and strength.

- **The Breath of the Divine (Unis, Gift of Life):**
    - **Metaphysical Purpose:** The breath symbolizes the divine spark within, continuously renewing the Ka and keeping it aligned with cosmic life forces.
    - **Application:** Practice deep, intentional breathing, imagining each inhale as divine light energizing your Ka and each exhale as a release of stagnation.
- **The Sacred Mirror (Teti, Reflection of the Divine):**
    - **Metaphysical Purpose:** The mirror represents self-awareness, showing the Ka as a reflection of divine perfection and infinite potential.
    - **Application:** <u>Visualize yourself gazing into a luminous mirror,</u> seeing your Ka radiant with divine energy and purpose.

Deployment: Phrases and Symbolism

- Use affirmations such as: *"My Ka is radiant and strong, sustained by the eternal life force of the divine."*
- Visualize golden streams of light and sacred breaths to empower your Ka.

- Symbols include mirrors, breath, and energy streams as representations of the divine self.

Practical Insight for Empowering the Ka: The Spells for Empowering the Ka remind the SUNs of God that their vitality and divine nature are inexhaustible. By energizing their Ka, they maintain the strength to face challenges and embrace their spiritual journey.

22. Sacred Union: Merging with Divine Completeness

The **Spells for Sacred Union** celebrate the ultimate goal of the soul's journey: the integration of all polarities and the realization of divine wholeness. These spells emphasize unity between the physical and spiritual, masculine and feminine, and light and shadow. For the SUNs of God, sacred union is the profound merging of the self with the divine, a state of eternal completeness and harmony.

Key Spells and Metaphysical Interpretation:

- **The Two Horizons (Pepi II, Balance of Heaven and Earth):**
    - **Metaphysical Purpose:** The two horizons symbolize the unity of opposites—masculine and feminine, light and shadow—creating a harmonious whole.
    - **Application:** Meditate on the image of the rising and setting sun, feeling the balance of polarities within you.

- **The Embrace of Nut and Geb (Unis, Cosmic Union):**

    - **Metaphysical Purpose:** This spell reflects the merging of earth and sky, a metaphor for the integration of material and spiritual realms.
    - **Application:** <u>Visualize yourself embraced by Nut (the heavens) and Geb (the earth),</u> uniting all aspects of your being in divine harmony.

- **The Knot of Isis (Teti, Seal of Connection):**

    - **Metaphysical Purpose:** The knot represents unbreakable connections, symbolizing the soul's eternal bond with the divine.
    - **Application:** <u>Visualize a glowing knot of light binding you to the divine source,</u> a reminder of your inseparable unity with creation.

Deployment: Phrases and Symbolism

- Use affirmations such as: ***"I am whole and complete, united with the divine in eternal harmony."***
- Visualize celestial embraces, radiant knots, and balanced horizons.
- Symbols include knots, horizons, and divine pairs to reflect sacred union.

Practical Insight for Sacred Union:
The Spells for Sacred Union guide the SUNs of God to integrate all aspects of their being. This stage celebrates the soul's realization of divine completeness and eternal connection to the source.

23. Mastering Cosmic Law: Living in Alignment

The **Spells for Mastering Cosmic Law** emphasize the importance of aligning with Ma'at—the embodiment of truth, justice, and harmony. These spells serve as a guide for the SUNs of God to live ethically and spiritually in balance with universal principles. By mastering cosmic law, the seeker integrates divine wisdom into their daily life, creating a foundation for spiritual growth and harmony.

Key Spells and Metaphysical Interpretation:

- **The Words of Ma'at (Pepi I, Divine Truth):**
    - **Metaphysical Purpose:** This spell aligns the soul with Ma'at, embodying truth, justice, and harmony. It serves as a guide for ethical and spiritual living.
    - **Application:** Reflect on the principles of Ma'at, affirming your commitment to truth and integrity in every thought, word, and action.

- **The Cosmic Scales (Unis, Balance of the Universe):**
    - **Metaphysical Purpose:** The scales represent the soul's accountability to cosmic law, emphasizing balance and fairness in all aspects of life.
    - **Application:** <u>Visualize your heart being weighed against Ma'at's feather,</u> affirming your dedication to living in alignment with universal principles.
- **The Divine Oath (Teti, Vow of Harmony):**
    - **Metaphysical Purpose:** This spell emphasizes the power of intention and commitment, binding the soul to its highest purpose.
    - **Application:** Declare your divine intentions aloud, affirming your alignment with cosmic truth and harmony.

Deployment: Phrases and Symbolism

- Use affirmations such as: ***"I walk in harmony with Ma'at, living by divine truth and universal law."***
- Visualize cosmic scales and oaths of light to reinforce your alignment with Ma'at.

- Symbols include scales, feathers, and sacred vows, representing balance and commitment.

Practical Insight for Mastering Cosmic Law:
The Spells for Mastering Cosmic Law guide the SUNs of God to live in harmony with universal principles. This stage emphasizes the importance of ethical integrity and spiritual alignment in achieving divine mastery.

24. Eternal Radiance: Becoming the Light

The **Spells for Eternal Radiance** guide the SUNs of God to embrace their divine nature as sources of light and inspiration. These spells emphasize the soul's transformation into a beacon of truth, love, and wisdom, radiating its essence throughout the cosmos. By becoming the light, the seeker fulfills their highest purpose, inspiring others to ascend and align with divine truth.

Key Spells and Metaphysical Interpretation:

- **The Radiance of Ra (Pepi II, Beacon of Light):**
    - **Metaphysical Purpose:** This spell invokes the eternal light of Ra, guiding the soul to shine as a beacon of divine truth and love.
    - **Application:** Visualize yourself bathed in Ra's golden light, radiating warmth, wisdom, and compassion to all beings.

- **The Starry Crown (Unis, Cosmic Illumination):**
    - **Metaphysical Purpose:** The starry crown symbolizes enlightenment and the soul's ascension to its rightful place among the divine.
    - **Application:** <u>Visualize yourself wearing a crown of stars,</u> each representing a divine attribute you embody.
- **The Eternal Flame (Teti, Light of the Infinite):**
    - **Metaphysical Purpose:** The flame signifies the soul's immortality and its power to inspire and uplift others.
    - **Application:** Meditate on a flame burning within your heart, growing brighter as you align with your divine purpose.

Deployment: Phrases and Symbolism

- Use affirmations such as: ***"I am the eternal light, illuminating the path of truth and love."***
- Visualize radiant crowns, flames, and suns to embody eternal radiance.

- Symbols include light, stars, and flames as metaphors for divine illumination.

Practical Insight for Eternal Radiance:
The Spells for Eternal Radiance remind the SUNs of God that their ultimate purpose is to embody and share divine light. By becoming a beacon of truth, the soul fulfills its highest potential and inspires others to ascend.

25. Unity with the Source: The Ultimate Return

The **Spells for Unity with the Source** lead the SUNs of God to the culmination of their spiritual journey—complete oneness with the divine source. These spells emphasize the dissolution of all dualities and the soul's return to its eternal origin. By merging with the infinite light, the seeker transcends individuality and becomes part of the eternal cycle of creation.

Key Spells and Metaphysical Interpretation:

- **The Path of the Eternal SUN (Pepi II, Merging with Ra):**
    - **Metaphysical Purpose:** This spell represents the final stage of ascension, where the soul merges fully with Ra, the divine source of all creation.
    - **Application:** <u>Visualize yourself as a ray of sunlight returning to its source.</u> Feel the warmth and unity of merging with infinite light and divine love.

- **The Circle of Eternity (Unis, Unbroken Unity):**
    - **Metaphysical Purpose:** The circle symbolizes the soul's eternal nature, unending and inseparable from the cosmic order.
    - **Application:** Meditate on a golden circle surrounding you, representing your oneness with the divine and the infinite cycle of existence.
- **The Embrace of Atum (Teti, Completion of the Journey):**
    - **Metaphysical Purpose:** Atum represents the all-encompassing divine energy, drawing all aspects of creation into unity. This spell signifies the soul's final embrace of divine completeness.
    - **Application:** Imagine being embraced by a radiant, all-encompassing light that dissolves all boundaries, leaving only pure being.

Deployment: Phrases and Symbolism

- Use affirmations such as: ***"I return to the source, one with the infinite light of creation."***
- Visualize radiant circles, sunlight, and divine embraces as metaphors for unity.
- Symbols include circles, suns, and radiant light representing the ultimate union with the source.

Practical Insight for Unity with the Source:

The Spells for Unity with the Source guide the SUNs of God to their final destination—oneness with the divine. This stage represents the completion of the soul's journey, where all dualities dissolve, and the SUN becomes an eternal part of the infinite light.

The Sacred Journey of the SUNs of God

The **Pyramid Texts** represent an ancient, profound blueprint for spiritual evolution, charting the soul's journey through realms of transformation, illumination, and ultimate unity with the divine. Through these spells, the SUNs of God are offered not just tools for navigating the metaphysical realms, but a cohesive roadmap for their sacred journey toward enlightenment and self-realization.

Each spell serves as a stepping stone, designed to elevate the soul by guiding it through the various dimensions of consciousness. From protection and purification to empowerment and divine ascension, these stages mirror the timeless truth that growth, transformation, and enlightenment are the birthright of every being.

The Journey in Stages

The path begins with foundational spells for grounding and protection, creating the space for the soul to move beyond fear and resistance. As the journey unfolds, the seeker is empowered to embrace divine wisdom, invoke higher consciousness, and align with cosmic order.

The middle phases focus on harmonizing the inner and outer worlds, forging unity between light and shadow, and recognizing the sacredness of duality. Finally, the spells for ascension and unity elevate the seeker to the highest realms of being, where all limitations dissolve into the infinite light of divine oneness.

Practical Integration

The Pyramid Texts remind us that the soul's journey is not confined to any one life or time. The spells are eternal keys, available to be unlocked at any stage of spiritual development. By engaging with these teachings—through visualization, intention, and the application of ancient wisdom—modern seekers can access the profound truths embedded in these texts.

The journey is cyclical, and the tools provided are meant to be revisited throughout the soul's eternal progression. Whether one is just beginning the path or approaching its culmination, the insights offered in this work inspire the SUNs of God to rise beyond limitations, embrace their divine heritage, and embody the infinite light of creation.

Metaphysical Translation of the Resurrection Ritual

In the ancient Pyramid Texts, the resurrection ritual speaks not of physical rites alone but of the eternal processes of the soul's awakening and elevation. The "invocation of Geb" reflects the grounding of the Higher Self into divine order. Geb, as the archetype of the Earthly Father, represents the stabilizing force of creation, calling forth the latent potential within the fragmented self to rise into spiritual awareness. His presence invites the soul to recognize its connection to the foundational aspects of existence while aspiring toward the divine.

The resurrection itself becomes a metaphysical rebirth, where the divine essence of Osiris within each of us reclaims its sovereignty. The "keening falcon" mentioned in the Pyramid Texts symbolizes the soul's ascension through Horus's divine eye, where vision pierces the veils of illusion. The falcon, tied to celestial sight, guides the resurrected spirit from darkness into the illumination of higher consciousness. The repeated invocations in the text represent the soul's affirmations, each "recitation" a call to reclaim its divine legacy.

As one of the texts describe, "Pepi Neferkare will be born there," the birth is not one of flesh but of divine identity, where the Higher Self reawakens to its eternal truth. This rebirth signifies the transcendence of physical mortality, a resurrection of consciousness into the eternal light of the Akhet.

The Metaphysical Role of Isis and Nephthys: Integration of Divine Wisdom and Healing

In the commending of Isis and Nephthys, the Pyramid Texts illustrate the interplay of two archetypes essential for the reconstitution of the fragmented soul. Isis embodies divine wisdom, the active force of love that seeks out and integrates the scattered aspects of the Higher Self. Her weeping reflects the soul's longing for unity, while her gathering of Osiris's pieces symbolizes the meticulous work of self-awareness and healing. Isis transforms sorrow into wholeness, embodying the alchemical process of turning loss into spiritual gold.

Nephthys, as the hidden counterpart to Isis, represents the unseen, protective forces that cradle the soul during its darkest moments. She is the silent guardian of transition, holding space for the soul's resurrection. Together, Isis and Nephthys create a balance between action and receptivity, reminding the Suns of God that spiritual transformation requires both the active pursuit of truth and the quiet surrender to divine timing.

The lamentation described in the Pyramid Texts is not one of despair but of release—a purging of the attachments and illusions that bind the soul to the material. This "weeping" is a catharsis, an acknowledgment of the necessary dissolution before reassembly. Through their combined efforts, Isis and Nephthys restore Osiris to a state of divine completeness, offering a profound lesson in the power of integration.

Establishing the Spirit as Osiris: The Crown of Divine Sovereignty

The establishment of the spirit as Osiris marks the culmination of the resurrection ritual, where the soul fully embodies its divine identity. Osiris, as the archetype of kingship, represents the sovereignty of the Higher Self over the inner kingdom. To "establish" the spirit as Osiris is to crown the soul with the authority of divine consciousness, aligning every aspect of being with the eternal.

The Pyramid Texts describe the "wings of Geb" as the grounding force that enables this ascension. Geb's embrace symbolizes the firm foundation needed for the soul to rise into its highest potential. This establishment is not merely a declaration but a process of mastery, where the soul integrates the lessons of fragmentation, reassembly, and resurrection into a unified state of divine awareness.

As the texts proclaim, "Your ties have been loosened by Nu's Two Lords," the soul is released from the binds of duality and illusion, entering the oneness of divine truth. The spirit, now established as Osiris, stands as a beacon of light, embodying the eternal principles of balance, justice, and divine order.

The Resurrection Ritual and the Zodiacal Planes

The five epagomenal days, mentioned within the context of Osiris's resurrection, are revisited here as bridges that align the fragmented self with the higher planes of existence. Each day correlates with a step in the resurrection process, guiding the soul through physical, emotional, mental, causal, and spiritual integration.

- **Day One (Physical Plane)**: The foundation where the soul confronts its material existence, recognizing the body as a vessel for divine expression.
- **Day Two (Emotional Plane)**: The release of attachments and the purification of the heart, mirroring the balance of the scales in Ma'at's teachings.
- **Day Three (Mental Plane)**: The clarity of thought and alignment of the mind with higher wisdom, symbolized by the piercing gaze of Horus.
- **Day Four (Causal Plane)**: The realization of the soul's karmic journey and its role within the divine order.
- **Day Five (Spiritual Plane)**: The crowning of the spirit as Osiris, fully integrated and aligned with the eternal.

Conclusion: The Metaphysical Journey of Resurrection

The resurrection ritual, as laid out in the Pyramid Texts, is more than a series of invocations or rites. It is a map for the Suns of God to navigate their own spiritual journeys. From the grounding of Geb to the gathering forces of Isis and Nephthys, to the crowning of Osiris, each step reveals a profound truth about the soul's path to enlightenment.

By understanding these texts metaphysically, we see that resurrection is not an event but a process—a continual unfolding of divine awareness. The Suns of God are called not only to witness this resurrection but to embody it, becoming Osiris in their own right. Through the integration of wisdom, healing, and sovereignty, you step into your eternal nature, carrying forth the legacy of light and truth that Osiris represents.

Your Role as a SUN of God

As a SUN of God, you carry the eternal spark of divinity within you. This roadmap calls you to awaken to your divine potential, recognizing that every challenge, revelation, and transformation along the path serves your greater ascent. The Pyramid Texts show that the journey through the realms of light and shadow is the sacred work of returning to your divine essence.

Let this work inspire you to explore the depths of your consciousness, to honor the divine in yourself and others, and to rise as a beacon of enlightenment. The journey through the cycles and portals is not just a passage—it is a profound calling to embody your role as a co-creator in the divine plan.

Final Affirmation

"I embrace my sacred journey as a SUN of God. Through light and shadow, I rise toward divine unity, embodying the eternal truth of my divine essence."

www.ingramcontent.com/pod-product-compliance
Lightning Source LLC
Chambersburg PA
CBHW070734230426
43665CB00016B/2242